THE WINTER WITHIN

BOOK OF POEMS

ARUN SADASIVAN

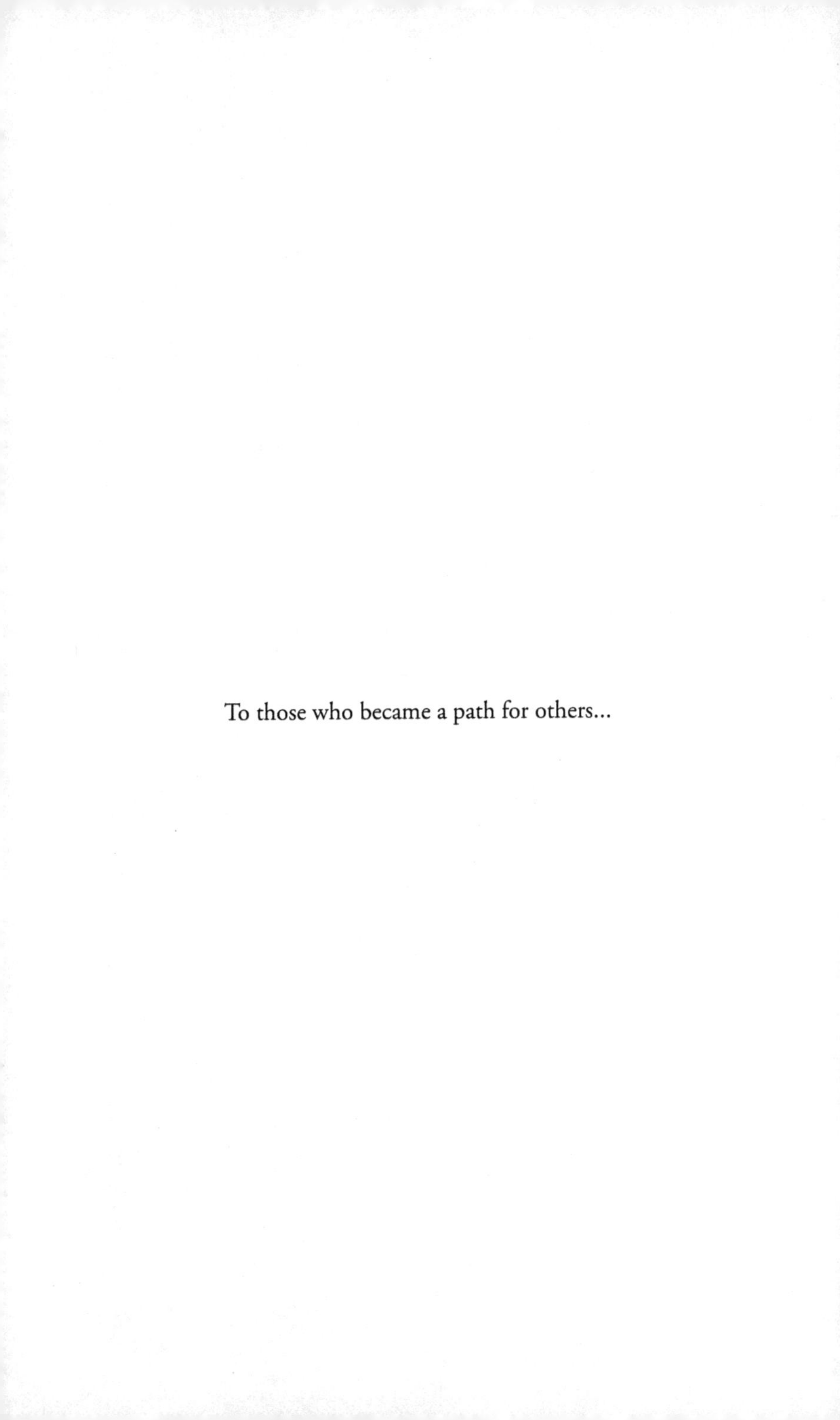

To those who became a path for others...

Contents

Contents

Contents

Foreword

Every winter contains within itself a promise of spring, a time of life and love. Though the winter could be prolonged or severe, this promise is infallible and definite. Every living thing waits for its arrival with hope and longing. Though the winter is painful and dreaded, its departure leaves one with a certain unexplainable nostalgia of a time that was resisted and undesired, yet necessary and inevitable. Especially when one realises how it helped sustain and nurture that hope and love which is incarnated in spring.

This collection of poems by Dr. Arun Sadasivan, is a spontaneous articulation of the winter that is pregnant with the seeds of a beautiful spring. Though the undesired winter, which is the reality of human existence is often painful and paradoxical or even contradictory, often carries with it the seeds of meaning and purpose necessary for a fleeting existence; and provides it the needed impetus to continue and exist. A reading through these poems brings to mind the pain of winter but a distant and sure hope of a beautiful spring, bustling with life and energy.

This simple but meaningful articulations are laced with the smell of earth, life and humanity, untouched by superfluity and cosmetic decorations of meaningless words. They are natural as they can be and as fresh as the first blade of grass on the field. While the author meanders around the nooks and corners of life that is unattractive as a fearsome winter, he takes notice of a reality that is bare and potent. He pens his witness in ways that is understandable and experienceable to souls untouched by the myopia of self-centeredness and narcissism.

This book is a sure experience of moments, memories, thoughts, feelings, and awareness of the simplicity of life, relationships, and a journey inevitable to every soul.

Fr Tomy Joseph

Acknowledgements

I acknowledge everyone who kindled my thoughts and imagination.

1. Our Life

• 1 •

Life holds much meaning
When it is defined by
Someone special in our life...
Yet, we call it Our Life
(June 2020)

2. Life flows…

Sometimes
In life, we find,
Despite our successes,
Failure lingers.
Though we know this,
Still, we play.
We play so well,
And, gracefully accept failure.
(October 2020)

3. Blissful Art

I became a word in the poem,
Words lined up as they came,
With no control over what would follow.
I didn't know what I inscribed,
I just listened to the words that floated,
Blending with the true rhythm,
And, becoming part of the creator.
Divinity bestowed upon me
The patience to wait until the end
To realise what flowed through me
The beauty of creation
Left me awestruck
The touch of a real artist.
I never knew it.
I could never have made it.
When I pen down, words flow through my fingers;
I just move my hand, guided by my mind
The process is wonderful,
I realised I am also HIS art.
Ecstatic in my journey
Beatific in my search of Art
Every creation derived directly,
With no worries along the way.

(June 2020)

4. Memories

Some memories are to cherish
They rejuvenate and kindle joy.
We love to remember them,
Though it is hard to recollect.
Some memories are painful
The ones we never want to remember,
Yet, lingers with us, always.
(October 2020)

5. You came as a message

• 6 •

You came as a message for me
A trigger, to break off my slave life.
I believed it was a life until you touched me.
Slept without warmth,
Ate without love,
Lived without life.
I ignored the rays of dawn,
Immersed myself in the darkness of dusk,
And believed, it was a life
Though I was searching for my existence
(November 2022)

6. Moments of Life

Every step in life is filled with
The pain of separation and
And the joy of togetherness
Still await the next moments.
(July 2020)

7. Desires

• 8 •

What I see in the mirror
Are the marks of my body.
Every Mark has a story
Story of my desires
And how desires leave their marks.
(June 2020)

8. Who begins your day?

The regular phone call,
A ritual from my dad.
It was from childhood
All through my life
Schools, colleges and workspaces.
It was a common landline call
Which I used to receive
Hardly for a minute or two.
Morning, every morning
I get energised
I felt connected
I longed for the familiar ring.
I never asked him
Why does he call me every morning.
He never explained,
I never felt irritating,
It was my call from the sun.
Now I feel upset
Because now it's my turn to make a call
But I am busy with work.
My father was never busy
He was working for us,
Remembering us every time.

But Now I have failed,
To do what I am supposed to do.
(June 2020)

9. A second life

• 11 •

Everyone starts feeling the life
After a short death during their lifetime.
Start cherishing their rebirth,
Feel the fullness of life,
They dance, sing, pray,
And celebrate every morning.
A few, overwhelmed with love
Stand still at sunrise, and embrace the warmth.
They start experiencing the grace in all beings,
And a beautiful nature born within them.
(January 2021)

10. The silent walk

I cherish wandering at night,
Leaving everything behind,
And setting on an endless walk.
untouched by emotions, with no baggage.
In my absence, I could see an anxious face
Wandering everywhere
In search of me.
I couldn't tolerate it -
Held my breath,
Came back to my bed
And slept again.
(February 2021)

11. Love unspoken

Travelled thousands of kilometres
To give her a kiss
But, I wanted to give it on the forehead
When her eyes were open.
(February 2021)

12. Story of Colours

• 14 •

Colours were beautiful

Until people started owning colours.

Colours are segregated into identities, feelings and emotions.

The sight of some colour

Upsets us,

Makes us feel happy,

Makes us feel angry.

A colour can condition us,

And even predict us.

(March 2021)

13. Spelling Mistakes

•15•

I like spelling mistakes.
When I read someone's writings,
I could see my friend there.
I can read his writings
Without teasing him
Because only we know
What it meant to us.
(March 2021)

14. King

King without Kingdom
King without Servants
King without Power
Still, I am a King
King of my life
My life.
(May 2021)

15. Fear to write again

The most painful messages are
The condolences messages.
Becoming part of everyday life during this Covid.
Every time I write a message
My hands are shivering.
The first one was for a known celebrity,
Then it was for friend's family,
Then it was for an aged teacher,
Again it was for my colleague,
Once again for a distant family member,
Now, I am writing for my student.
It is becoming very close to me
I am scared to write again.
My hands are trembling with fear.
How many more I should write
my deepest condolences
Until someone writes for me.
(June 2021)

16. Life

Life is uncertain and infinite
Both give us two options :
Either to celebrate each moment
Or, worry every second.
It's up to us to decide
How we will embrace our life.
(September 2021)

17. A drop of silence

• 19 •

Silence is not anger.

It is not negative.

It is as important.

or more important, than words.

It is easy to absord words

when you listen to silence.

You absord words and more.

It is a language of nature.

It is a language of breath.

.Just absorb it as it pours into you.

A drop of silence...

(July 2024)

18. The Winter within

Not smiled
While giving.
Not cherished
While hugging.
Not melted
While kissing.
Not looked at eyes
While holding.
Not felt respected
While asking.
Not felt cared for
While thrusting.
Not felt loved
While being loved.
Then, its human-
Only they can.
(July 2024)

19. Unconditionally

Never tell me you're old,
Because I never loved your age.
Never tell me you're ugly,
Because I never loved your appearance.
Never tell me you're fat,
Because I never loved your shape.
You are shapeless, beautiful,
flowing thoughts.
I just love your thoughts.
Stimulating my mind with
your infinite waves.
Until I finished reading you,
I was blind.
I read you unconditionally.
You illuminated my mind,
Showed me beyond the familiar path.
You gave me the gut to follow you
For the rest of my life.
(December 2018)

20. Sailing together

My words may create guilt in you,
But our togetherness creates happiness.
Let us be happy when we are together.
Let us communicate through silence,
Let us wander in this unnamed world
Until we find a different path
That leads to our destiny.
Till then, let us travel together,
To find the meaning of this life.
We together carved a path,
Delving into the depths of mind.
I became your student,
And you led me to another world.
We gathered words to explain what we felt.
but it was never audible.
Futile attempts to convince
Never worried us about shattered voices.
We held together, and walk further
Sailing into the waves of life,
Together.
(December 2018)

21. The day before death

Let me leave everyone
Let me stop worrying
Let me stop caring
Let me become selfish -
Just for a day.
I was busy caring everyone
Everyone loved me,
Respected me
and were happy in my presence.
I was running for everyone
Till the day before I died.
Now, I have one more day.
I wish to be selfish
Before I leave this life.
I cut my nails,
Held my heart,
Spent some time with myself.
Stood before the mirror,
Watched sunrise and sunset
Touched water and mud again -
Before they cover me.
My day was beautiful
Not bothered about anyone.

They will be happy even after I'm gone.
I can't resist the inevitable.
And I'm happy with this day.
Let me leave tomorrow
With this beautiful memory.
(January 2019)

22. When hearts speak

I am near you,
Watching you sleep.
I could not feel
to leave you alone.
Pressing your hands,
Now I feel calm -
I hope you do too.
Let me take your pain,
Your worries, your heaviness.
Let me listen to your voice,
Your mind,
Your heart.
Arguing for life,
Asking for a chance,
Crying for time.
Tears fell from my eyes
For your pain.
I kissed your forehead.
You held me close,
To be with you
You fell into a deep sleep,
Your hearts melting,
Thoughts fading,

Voice disappearing.
You are calm now,
With the hoope of tomorrow.
And now, let me sleep too.
(January 2019)

23. Being Naked

I was naked in your eyes
When you were my mother
I was naked on your shoulder
When you were my father
I was naked in your feet
When you were my grandparent
I was naked in your mind
When you were my soulmate
I was naked in your heart
When you were my friend
I was naked in your hand
When you were my nurse
I was naked in your life
When you were my destiny
I was naked in your lap
When you were my death
(February 2019)

24. Whispers of comfort

I am not your guardian,
I am not your teacher,
I am not your mind.
If you follow your guardian
You may reach the beautiful destiny
It may fulfil all your needs
It may give you comfort in life.
If you follow your teacher
You may reach the insightful destiny
Filled with knowledge,
You may get much acceptance.
If you follow your mind
You may get wisdom
Meaning in life,
And surround yourself with followers.
If you follow me,
We need to walk together.
We may reach a destiny
Filled with love and life.
Filled with pain and peace.
And it may quench the thirst of your soul.
(February 2019)

25. Layers of bonding

I still have-
Mind to hold your pain,
Blood to carry your heart,
Breath to give you life,
Amd soul to be with you.
No more can you touch me
Or sense me with your eyes.
You can feel me in your breath,
Hear my heartbeat.
I disappeared into the mud,
And reborn as you within you.
Ever to be with you-
No one can stop us.
I see you every day,
Breath through you,
Live my life in you.
Being within you,
I feel your pain
And I shall hold it for you.
(February 2019)

26. Big or small

Wish to be big-
Big like Dad,
Big like Teacher,
Big like Brother.
Only to be Big.
When I get Big,
Big become Bigger.
Big never enjoyed Small.
Small was Bigger.
When I am Big,
Big is no more
fascinating.
Now, Small is my wish.
(February 2019)

27. In the arms of God

If you see my colour
When I am in love,
If you check my strength
When I am sick,
If you test my tolerance
When I am in pain,
If you doubt my work
When I am at service,
If you check my patience
When I am curious,
If you make me wait
When I am eager to see you,
I always wish to say no -
A big no to you God.
Oh God, you always
Delayed and made me
More resilient, more humane.
I was moulded in your arms,
Risking myself to find the treausre of life.
(February 2019)

28. Unspoken Love

• 32 •

You may not have stories
for me; not even words
Still, I love to listen to your breath-
They tell your love for me
In your silence.
(July 2020)

29. Sinking in her tears

I sink into a drop;
It was big enough to engulf me.
I swam to survive
Till my last breath.
When I opened my eyes,
A tear rested on my face.
She was crying,
Missing me,
Even as I lay in her lap,
Too far away to see.
I saw her when I wished,
But she misses me every day.
I sink into her tears
Each time she cries for me.
(August 2020)

30. Wired Connections

• 34 •

I listen to songs with you,
Feel the tickle of your hair,
The soft-touch of your feathers
Between your breaths.
I love listening with you
Through old wired earphones
That connects us.
The more ties it has,
The closer we are.
The shorter the wire,
The more she leaned on my shoulder.
I wish it were even shorter,
With many knots in it.
She hums for me,
Being so close to me.
Even though she gifted me new
Wireless earphones,
She kept the old one
To share her songs as always.
(August 2020)

31. The circle of life

• 35 •

Life is infinite-
No ending,
No beginning,
No one is first,
No one is last.
But we shape it-
It is the circle of life.
(August 2020)

32. Swapping emotions

• 36 •

When I replace emotions,
I really don't wish to swap -
But I am forced to.
When I am sad,
They wish to see me smile.
When I am happy,
They expect my sadness.
When I am angry,
They expect my silence.
Swapping since childhood,
I have still not learned it properly.
When the time comes,
I will need to swap your absence.
I was broken,
Realising you are my emotion.
You can't be substituted,
You can't be swapped.
It hurts, truly.
(January 2021)

33. I live in her

Live in her eyes
When she cries.
Live in her whisper
When she prays.
Live in her hands
When she feeds.
Live in her lips
When she sings.
Live in her feet
When she loves.
Live in her lap
When she pampers.
Live in her neck
When she hugs.
Live in her mind
When she devotes.
I found myself,
Lost for many years,
Lost in many places.
I live in her
More than I live in myself.
(January 2020)

34. Being sensitive

Painful to see a man hurting another
Yet, everyone celebrates
Posting it as their status
It became status -
The pain of a fellow being.
It doesn't matter who is right or wrong
Just see the two human beings
Then, it will be painful to witness.
We conditioned our brain
to find good and bad.
Justifying any hurt.
When we see it as police and public
We feel okey, even entertained.
But he does not commit crimes
By merely being human.
We might feel okey
until we experience it.
Teach our brain to see pain as pain
A chance to help ourselves
And, to become sensitive.
(March 2020)

35. Heal Ourselves

Illness is a window,
A window to our own life.
It gives us time for ourselves.
We become natural,
As simple as our smell.
Minimal people accompany us -
No one stay forever...
Most of the time, we are alone.
The solitude makes us sensitive
We start observing ourselves.
We can't tolerate pain -
Yet, pain is light.
Focus on your pain
And the bosy part
will become our centre of attention.
Until the pain engulfs us,
We never though about
The beautiful machine we have.
We never took the time to care it.
Pain teaches us unconditional awareness
Awareness becomes medicine
The pain take us to that awareness
We focus on the body, the pain.

We become more aware of self
Gradually, we heal our pain
Our attention heals us
Our awareness heals us.
(March 2020)

36. I am a bird

I always forget -
I can't fly,
I can't sing,
But I am a bird.
I do not have
Beautiful feathers
Or a colourful tail,
Still, I am a bird.
I see what you see -
Sunrise, sunset,
Moonlight, blue sky -
But I can't fly
Still, I am a bird.
I can feel
Pain and happiness,
Teasing and bullying,
But I won't cry
Because I belong to you all.
I may fly tomorrow,
I may sing tomorrow,
But I have to live today
So, I forget what I can't.
I know that if I say I can't,

You will all throw me out.
And then I will fall into death.
But, I wish to live,
So I forget easily,
Be with all of you
I am a strong bird.
(April 2019)

37. Poetic healing

Words flow from my heart,
I can't tell them to anyone,
But only I can scribble.
Each time I scribble, I feel calm;
It is a delightful medication.
If I don't do this,
I might lose my rhythm of life.
And I must never forget it.
Each line contains
The sweetness of teh darkness
The pain of brightness.
Every time, hope is weaved through words,
Every drop of energy being used
To describe the pain of life.
It also brings some energy to write.
Continue the process of healing -
A poet can heal himself,
And when we read, it will heal us.
Writing is a beautiful process,
Enabling daring moves to share.
All poems heal me
They may heal you as well.
(June 2020)

38. Echoes of pain

Give me some thorns;
I want to gift them to many.
A few are not enough;
I need many thorns.
I want to multiply the thorns in me,
To give away as gifts.
First, I wish to give them
To those who gave me the name
'Fatty pig', although I was chubby.
Then to my classmates in
the sixth grade,
who made a song
that echoed the shaming of my body.
Also, I wish to throw them to
Whoever comes to help me
As they were more cruel
Than the people who hurt me.
(June 2020)

39. The colour of pain

What is the colour of pain?
It is a very bright colour.
It is not dark,
As I have heard from many.
It is a bright colour;
It holds many colours together.
Different for everyone,
Someone will come near
As they cannot resist.
Your colour attract them,
But they never think about it -
What they can really do
They just jump into our pain.
They stay with us till we heal.
It is a beautiful colour
That everyone holds
Yet, it is filled with so much pain.
(June 2020)

40. Life is grace

Graceful grace,
Experienced on your path
When shared, it multiplies.
You showed us how to
Touch many in our path
With the grace of divinity.
Grace is divine;
It can experience everywhere-
Not just within four walls,
Not just in any prayer hall.
It is only experienced through action.
The grace we feel
Comes when we connect with life.
Walking through all the thorns of existence.
When we have everything,
We rarely experience it -
Occupied with counting,
Obsessing over more.
Grace is experienced in a hospital:
From th etreating doctor,
A fellow donor,
Or a compassionate touch.
Anyone can make you feel grace.

Even a child can help you experience

The grace of the life that we have.

Yet, we fail to share it

Unless it is an absolute necessity.

We have become selfish in humanity.

Grace is a very sensitive ability of being.

It creates compassion and kindness.

Helping us love those who are suffering.

It resides inside our hearts

We speak about it.

But once we experience it,

We are transformed.

We can craete the same experience for many.

Having grace in our life leads to -

Being a source of grace in others lives

Passing grace to humanity,

Sustaining it forever in our hearts

Life is grace, as always.

(June 2020)

41. Shades of relationship

We were strangers,
Respectful and considerate.
Books brought us together.
We decided to live within them.
We read many books,
Lived through countless characters.
When we grew closer,
We stopped respecting each other.
We stopped considering each other.
Gradually, the books disappeared
And then, so did we.
Finally, we became strangers again -
Just like our first meeting.
This time, we didn't look at each other,
We chose to remain strangers,
To respect each other for the rest of our lives.
We are strangers.
(June 2020)

42. The beauty of life

Life gives you what you want.
It is just like being on the road.
If you are on a bicycle,
You need only that much space.
You move easily within it,
Happily, not bothered
By how big other vehicles are.
You focus only on what you have.
When you drive bigger vehicles.
The same road feels just as occupied.
Yet, you still find space to move furher.
It doesn't matter how big or small -
Life gives you what you seek.
Life will give you more if you seek.
Our duty is to wish
As much as we can.
You can fly your own flight,
Expanding into an infinite space.
That's the beauty of life -
Its shadow, and its truth.
(June 2020)

43. The waves of joy

It comes to us through the windows,
When we open them,
Through awareness.
Being aware of our life,
Serenity is what we experience,
With each second.
When we breath,
That's the way of joy -
The waves of joy.
(June 2020)

44. Attachment

It is a beautiful snake in life;
Sometimes, it becomes a burden.
You may feel the weight -
When it moves, it irritates.
We enjoy it most of teh time;
You feel its company,
Always with you,
Even if you don't require it.
You love to hold when it supports,
But, you wish to leave when it becomes a burden.
Its painful to leave
Struggling to hold on.
(June 2020)

45. Fragments of the heart

I am broken into pieces,
And left in many places.
One day, she will collect them
and fix it together.
That will be the best piece of art
Ever known to human life.
Each parts of me reveals
The thorns I received in my life.
Some parts I gifted to some
To ensure that they are happy forever.
Some parts were cut and taken
To secure their lives on this earth
Still; I am alive -
As good ,memories
And, as scary flashbacks.
But I am alive, as pieces,
To many hearts.
(June 2020)

About The Book

The Winter Within

Winter usually evokes images of cold, loneliness and gloom. But it is also a time to sit back, slow down, conserve energy, plunge into a deep meditative phase so as to rejuvenate with so much energy and vigour. It not just refreshes you physically, but engages you mentally. It resonates with the movement to make human life more meaningful by consciously slowing down and being reflective of our actions and engagements.

The poems in this collection depict winter as an image of resilience, hope and a meditative mind. Each poem is a meditative reflection of life, love, hope, emotions and relationships. The poetic beauty lies in the imagery and the subtle realities unearthed through the words.

About The Author

Arun Sadasivan is a poet, mental health professional and social worker with a decade and a half long engagement with children and disability. Having worked for different organisations and research institutes, he has rich experience in dealing with street children, children in conflict with law, children with genetic disorders, disability and children experiencing social and emotional issues. He led a national awareness and advocacy campaign 'Stepping Towards Equity' - An awareness walk for people living with Muscular Dystrophy across the state of Kerala, India in September 2023.

Arun's first book of poems 'Life Love Dreams' was published in 2021. He has published his poems in various magazines and journals including Muse India. Dr Arun Sadasivan is currently working as a children's social worker in the Royal Borough of Greenwich, London. He can be contacted at: dr.arunsadasivan@icloud.com.